TIMES
AND
SEASONS

TIMES
AND
SEASONS

Trusting God in Your Changing World

Trevor Newport

New Wine Press

New Wine Ministries
PO Box 17
Chichester
West Sussex
United Kingdom
PO20 6YB

Scripture quotations are taken from the following versions of the Bible:

The HOLY BIBLE, KING JAMES VERSION. Crown Copyright.

Author's emphasis is indicated by bold type

ISBN 1-903725-48-8

Typeset by CRB Associates, Reepham, Norfolk
Cover design by CCD, www.ccdgroup.co.uk
Printed in the United States of America

CONTENTS

INTRODUCTION

We all go through different seasons in our spiritual preparation, designed to refine our character. Some people seem to go through more than others, since they have many rough edges that need to be smoothed so as not to mar the purposes of God.

Whatever season you are going through right now, it will be for a reason which may or may not be obvious to you at this present time. Sometimes we get a glimpse of what the Lord is doing in our hearts and other times we are completely oblivious! I am sure that when we get to heaven the Lord will show us why we had to go through certain things and answer the questions we have long wanted answers for.

I pray that this book will help you to see the wider picture of God's kingdom and to realise that He is definitely in charge of your life as you seek His face and desire to go on with Him with all of your heart.

CHAPTER 1

NATURAL SEASONS

I have always loved the four seasons: Spring, Summer, Autumn and Winter. Each season brings something different and new. I like the way that during the change from Winter to Spring there is often quite an overlap before Spring is properly established. It can be difficult to know exactly what to wear during this time, since the temperature will go up and down even in one day! It is the sign of a seasonal change.

I have travelled much around the world and have to admit that, along with many in Britain, we take our seasons for granted. In some countries they do not have seasons in quite the same way that the UK does. I have been many times to Southern California on the west coast of the USA where the hot sun just keeps shining day after day! They are still wearing shorts and T shirts whilst having a barbeque on Christmas day! Then there is the other extreme: Northern Sweden and some parts of Canada get snow for up to six months a year!

I have come to appreciate my home country much more for having travelled so far.

It is Springtime at the time of writing and there are blossoms on many of the trees. It is such a glorious sight. Just a few weeks ago the trees were bare with no signs of fresh blossom at all. What a transformation! This change in season also seems to have an effect on people. I often think that people seem happier when the sun is shining! In England it rains a lot which tends to affect people in a negative way. You may be from a country where it is sunny for much of the time and rain is very welcome and everybody rejoices.

Spring then turns into Summer when we are supposed to get lots of sunshine! So is the theory. Some Summers have been so bad that you could hardly tell which season you were in! Thick black clouds can hang overhead for long periods and for many weeks at a time you don't see the sun at all!

Then comes Autumn when the trees start to shed their leaves. The colours change before they all fall off and it is often a spectacular sight to see. So many different shades of green, yellow and brown.

Then you wake up one morning and the car is covered with ice! You know that Winter has arrived and it is all change! You have to turn on the engine and let it run for ten minutes and scrape the ice off the windows (unless you have a garage of course!). The jumpers and pullovers come out along with hats and scarves etc.

The British seasons are certainly well defined and very different. There are different things to do in each season – each having its own purpose.

"While the earth remaineth, seedtime and harvest, and cold and heat, and summer and winter, and day and night shall not cease."

(GENESIS 8:22)

CHAPTER 2

A TIME TO
EVERY SEASON

"To every thing there is a season, and a time to every purpose under the heaven:

A time to be born, and a time to die; a time to plant, and a time to pluck up that which is planted;

A time to kill, and a time to heal; a time to break down, and a time to build up;

A time to weep, and a time to laugh; a time to mourn, and a time to dance;

A time to cast away stones, and a time to gather stones together; a time to embrace, and a time to refrain from embracing;

A time to get, and a time to lose; a time to keep, and a time to cast away;

A time to rend, and a time to sew; a time to keep silence, and a time to speak;

A time to love, and a time to hate; a time of war, and a time of peace."

(ECCLESIASTES 3:1–8)

I am sure that you can identify with many or all of the above as it covers much of life's experiences.

Let us look at childhood for a moment. According to many people that I have spoken to, when we are children time seems to stand still. When I was a child I did not think that I would ever grow older. Many people have a happy childhood with good parents and precious memories that often come back to them. However, so many people can testify to having had a very bad childhood for a multitude of reasons: the divorce of their parents, rejection by their mother or father, suffering physical abuse, sexual abuse, control, being spoilt, being made to do all the household chores, being ignored, etc. The list is endless. Having been a pastor for many years I have heard many stories of childhood problems that have been left unresolved for decades. Some people's lives are seemingly scarred for life because of their childhood years. However, Jesus can set you free from all trauma and abuse and give you completeness in Him. Hallelujah!

So for many that season was wonderful, but for others it was awful. I am glad that I had very caring parents who loved me and did their best for me, even though neither of my parents are Christians. I still have a great relationship with both of my parents, for which I am very grateful.

It seems that your upbringing plays a huge part in your life and either prepares you for, or hinders you in adulthood.

I have met so many people whose childhood was so poor that they have adopted a victim mentality. However, when you become a Christian, Jesus promises you victory in all areas of life! Therefore you are no longer a victim but a victor! Change your thinking!

> *"**For as he thinketh in his heart, so is he**: Eat and drink, saith he to thee; but his heart is not with thee."*
>
> (PROVERBS 23:7)

> *"And be not conformed to this world: but **be ye transformed by the renewing of your mind**, that ye may prove what is that good, and acceptable, and perfect, will of God."*
>
> (ROMANS 12:2)

You do not have to walk with a limp from your childhood for the rest of your life! There is freedom in Christ Jesus from all the things that the devil has stolen from you using other people. The first step is for you to forgive them. They were probably abused themselves by their parents and hurting people love to hurt others.

Ephesians 6:12 says,

> *"For we wrestle not against flesh and blood, but against principalities, against powers, against the rulers of the darkness of this world, against spiritual wickedness in high places."*

Our battle is not against people but the powers of darkness. We need to forgive people and cast out the devil's work.

Everybody needs releasing into freedom to one degree or another, so you are not the only one. Look at these verses in 1 Peter 5:

> *"Casting all your care upon him; for he careth for you. Be sober, be vigilant; because your adversary the devil, as a roaring lion, walketh about, seeking whom he may devour: Whom resist stedfast in the faith, **knowing that the same afflictions are accomplished in your brethren that are in the world.**"*
>
> (1 PETER 5:7–9)

When you are sitting next to someone in church you have no idea what kind of life they have endured or what they have been delivered of! People do not hang out dirty washing, but clean! The devil often lies to people about their life, saying that they are the only one to have gone through such trauma.

Having been in full-time ministry for twenty-five years and having dealt with many people, I have to admit that it seems that the majority of people have had problems in their childhood and those who had a good upbringing are in the minority.

Those of you who are bringing up children right now need to realise that what you put into your children now is so important and saves a lot of sorting out later!

Always speak positively to them and build them up with encouragement. Show them love every day and give discipline when it is needed, but love them straight after so that they are confident of your love for them. When I was a boy my friends used to be sent to their room when they did wrong and that only produces rejection. My mum or dad used to spank me and then love me which is the biblical way I believe.

Here is a wonderful verse of Scripture to comfort you if you have painful memories as a child:

> *"And I will restore to you the years that the locust hath eaten, the cankerworm, and the caterpiller, and the palmerworm, my great army which I sent among you."*
>
> (JOEL 2:25)

Your best years are ahead of you!

> *"But the path of the just is as the shining light, that shineth more and more unto the perfect day. The way of the wicked is as darkness: they know not at what they stumble."*
>
> (PROVERBS 4:18–19)

Here is another verse to help you to move on if the childhood season was bad:

> *"Brethren, I count not myself to have apprehended: but this one thing I do, forgetting those things which are behind, and reaching forth unto those things which are before."*
>
> (PHILIPPIANS 3:13)

Remember that you cannot change the past, but you can greatly affect the future by becoming an influence for righteousness, kindness, purity, and faith. But if you hold onto the hurts of the past, you will be an instrument to keep on hurting others, sometimes without you even being aware!

If you are going to enjoy the best seasons of your life, then you need to be grateful for what you do have and not to moan about what you don't have. We should live a life abounding in the praise of God all day long and expect God to change the things around us.

It is so hard to understand what purpose there was for having to go through bad things, but when you have been through a set of horrible circumstances you are able to empathise with others and come to their aid.

Why not pray and ask your heavenly Father to show you His purpose for a particular season or at least a glimpse this side of heaven. I have questions that I have asked God over the years that I know I shall not get the answer to until I see Him face to face. But I have learned not to allow my questions to create a stumbling block in my relationship and walk with God. I trust the Lord totally and do not allow my questions to prevent or hinder my service for Him. He knows everything and can see the whole picture, whereas we can only see our own little set of circumstances – often with tunnel vision at best!

Look at this verse:

"For the eyes of the Lord *run to and fro throughout the whole earth, to shew himself strong in the behalf of them whose heart is perfect toward him. Herein thou hast done foolishly: therefore from henceforth thou shalt have wars."*

(2 Chronicles 16:9)

CHAPTER 3

THE SEASON OF ADOLESCENCE

*"**Remember not the sins of my youth, nor my transgressions:** according to thy mercy remember thou me for thy goodness' sake, O LORD."*

(PSALM 25:7)

"For thou art my hope, O Lord GOD: thou art my trust from my youth."

(PSALM 71:5)

"Rejoice, O young man, in thy youth; and let thy heart cheer thee in the days of thy youth, and walk in the ways of thine heart, and

in the sight of thine eyes: but know thou, that for all these things
God will bring thee into judgment."

(ECCLESIASTES 11:9)

"Therefore remove sorrow from thy heart, and put away evil from
thy flesh: for childhood and youth are vanity."

(ECCLESIASTES 11:10)

"Remember now thy Creator in the days of thy youth,
while the evil days come not, nor the years draw nigh, when thou
shalt say, I have no pleasure in them."

(ECCLESIASTES 12:1)

There is an interesting difference between natural children and God's children. As we mature and "grow up", we find that we need to depend upon God more and more. But this is not so with natural children who, as they get older, become more and more independent of their parents. This is only right as they must develop into responsible adults one day. It is wrong to try to control young adults. They have to make their own decisions about the things of life. We should set the best example we can and trust that it will rub off on them. I was always grateful that my parents did not try to control me as I was getting older. I had to make my own decisions which I am glad of. We are responsible for our own actions in this life.

During the season of youth there are many changes that take place. We start to ask questions about life, death, God, what job we will do one day, our education and the opposite sex! It has to be the most challenging of all the seasons of life. It is challenging for parents to have to watch their children go through it. My children have just gone through adolescence and have thankfully come out shining for Jesus, for which Ruth and I are so grateful to God.

We have always been close as a family, but the inevitable happened when David (our eldest) decided to join the navy as a trainee officer. Ruth and I were quite concerned about his choice of job! We both sought the Lord and God spoke to both of us independently saying that he would come through it shining and that has come to pass. He spent three years training as an officer. We thought that the day he left would be the last that we would have him under our roof. How wrong we were! After three years he failed to pass a particular exam and was asked to leave. We were all quite shocked. A season was suddenly over for David completely unexpectedly. We have got used to having only our daughter Joy in the house and it is amazing how another person in the house makes such a difference!

So David has embarked on another season of his life; one which he certainly did not plan for. In fact many of the seasons that we find ourselves in are not planned at all! When I was a teenager, the very last job on earth that I would have chosen would have been to be a preacher! When I was sixteen I failed Religious Studies so badly that they threw me out of the class! Just four years later I was preparing for full-time ministry! Oh, how things can change in our lives! Not only does David have a new season, but we do too now that he is back with us in the family home. It is all change again! I think that Ruth feels it more than I do.

When David first came back home he was a bit unsettled and did not know what he should do or even where he should live. One minute he said one thing and the next minute he had changed his mind. It was a difficult "mini" season until he finally adjusted to life out of the navy. I am so glad that God spoke to me during this awkward season and it may help some readers. I did not know how to advise David on what he was doing and the Lord simply said these few words to my heart: "Just love him." That was all He said to me to do and so I did not try to tell him what to do, I just loved him. That is all we need to do sometimes when people are going through such a season. My relationship with him is now improving all the time for which I thank God. Maybe you need to step back and "just love" someone in your life right now? The late teens and early twenties are really important years and probably the most significant season for making the biggest decisions.

It is most interesting that we have to make the two most important decisions of our lives when we have the least experience – our career choice and the person that we will marry! So much thought and preparation needs to be put into these two areas of life.

When I was in my late teens, I decided to become an electronic engineer like my dad. But when I became a Christian I realised that I was making a big mistake and so I changed quickly. I was pursuing a career that I was not fit for at all! I don't know to this day why I thought that I could follow my dad's footsteps, since I was hopeless at physics! I even failed it at A level, which should have told me something. I was blind until Jesus came into my heart and I saw at once that I was heading in the wrong direction. How many people are in the wrong jobs, married to the wrong people and living in the wrong place? You can never fulfil your purpose or destiny on this Earth without knowing

Jesus Christ as your Lord and Saviour. If you do not know Him then call upon Him right now and ask Him to forgive you of your sin and ask Him to come into your heart. He promises to save all who will call upon Him.

"That if thou shalt confess with thy mouth the Lord Jesus, and shalt believe in thine heart that God hath raised him from the dead, thou shalt be saved. For with the heart man believeth unto righteousness; and with the mouth confession is made unto salvation. For the scripture saith, Whosoever believeth on him shall not be ashamed. For there is no difference between the Jew and the Greek: for the same Lord over all is rich unto all that call upon him. For whosoever shall call upon the name of the Lord shall be saved."

(ROMANS 10:9–13)

I am so glad that I found Jesus Christ at nineteen years of age. I wish that I had come to know Him much sooner! Many people find Jesus during their teen years, since it is a time when they are asking many questions about life.

It is truly a changing season with many challenges. If you have teenagers in your family, either children or grand-children, then you need to be patient with them and love them intently, letting them know that you are there for them. The worst thing that you can do is to nag them! It will drive them away. Remember that you were young once! Pray for them and trust that God will bring them through shining for Him and on the right path of righteousness and purity. Often the mistakes that we make early in life stand us in good stead for the future. It is one thing to listen to advice, but it is another to make a mistake and learn from it. The hardest lessons last the longest. When you have had your fingers burnt once you are very unlikely to let it happen again! Sometimes we have to sit back and watch people make mistakes and let them learn from them. It takes time for pride and arrogance to be driven out of us!

CHAPTER 4

THE SEASON OF YOUNG ADULTHOOD

I realise that everyone has a different life experience. Some marry young; some marry later in life; some don't get married at all. I can only speak from my own experience.

When I was twenty years old I met Ruth Hutchinson who later became Ruth Newport! We met and fell in love straight away and wanted to be married as quickly as possible. We courted for about eighteen months, which is something I would strongly recommend. You have to make sure that you want to spend the rest of your life with that person. I believe that courtship is a time to ask all the questions you need to about your partner. Don't assume that they will automatically want what you do just because you are in love! Ruth and I talked about everything: our past successes and failures, previous relationships, children, jobs etc. I am amazed when people come to me for advice in marriage because they have discovered something about their partner they had no knowledge of. "Did you not know that before you were married?" I often ask. Why don't people talk before they tie the knot? You need to know everything about the person you are marrying: their likes and dislikes, money matters, where to live, where to go to church etc. Don't assume anything! You have been warned!

Ruth and I were married and had children straight away. We married at twenty-two and had two children by the time we were twenty-four! To some that might seem very quick. But looking back I would not change that at all. Ruth agrees with me. Even though it was a struggle financially it was the most wonderful natural season of our lives. When David and Joy were young children we had so much fun. Ruth and I decided not to have a TV in the home for the first ten years of marriage so that we could devote our time to the children. We did not miss TV at all since we played games and had fun all the time.

I made a decision then that was to be one of the best decisions of my life. I was determined that I would do all of my work until the children came home from school each day and then I would spend quality time with them from four o'clock until six o'clock each day. I did that for years. I would not answer the phone or do any work at all, but focus on developing my relationship with each of my children. It was such a wonderful season for me as a father. I grew so close to both David and Joy. We would have a spiritual time together and also play games together. They were only one year apart in age and so they grew up very close to each other.

Even though we were living by faith, praying for our food most of the time, and trusting God for our needs to be met, it was a blessed season and so much fun. Ruth and I are reaping what we sowed those many years ago as our relationship with our children is so precious. At the time of writing David is almost twenty-three and Joy nearly twenty-two, and we are as close as ever.

It was a tough season however for Ruth, as she had come from living in a well-off family to be married to a pastor living by faith! Also, many people have a season when they are first married where they get to know each other without children. But David was conceived on our honeymoon, so we did not get much chance to get to know each other on our own.

There comes another season when the children start some serious study at school. "Not now dad!" became a familiar cry. I had to back off a lot from both our children since they both shone at school and both did well with four A levels each. That season of play with the children was gone for ever. It was a painful season for me as a father since I had been so close to both of them. It was at this time in my life that another season started and life would never be the same again!

I am in another season of my life now and looking forward to being a grandfather! Toys R Us here I come! I know that that season is going to be so much fun for me and Ruth, as we have loved parenthood so much. Being a grandparent must be even better fun, being able to wind up the children and then send them home to their parents! Hallelujah!

However, we have to be patient at the moment, since both of our children are still at home and are in a season themselves of being young adults, sorting out their careers and being on the lookout for their future spouse!

Life is certainly a series of ever-changing seasons, many of which flow into one another and overlap in so many ways. In fact the next season is often a consequence of the present one and how we come through it.

I am not qualified to speak about the next natural seasons since I have not lived through them yet! They would be middle age and old age. I am sure that they will have challenges of their own having spoken to many older people. I think that some seem to cope with growing older very well, but others seem to struggle. I must admit that even at the age of forty-six I am slowing down a bit and cannot keep up the kind of schedule that I have maintained over past years, so I have cut down on certain things – particularly flying internationally which has taken its toll over the years.

Maybe I will be able to write about middle and old age in a few years time!

CHAPTER 5

SHORT, MEDIUM AND LONG SEASONS

I have noticed in my life that we go through different types of seasons, both natural as well as spiritual. Some are short lived. For example Jesus was three days and three nights in the tomb until He rose from the dead. That was a short season in His life. It was absolutely necessary after He was crucified both to fulfil biblical prophecy as well as take on Satan single-handed to give us all authority over him.

29

"*Ye men of Israel, hear these words; Jesus of Nazareth, a man approved of God among you by miracles and wonders and signs, which God did by him in the midst of you, as ye yourselves also know: Him, being delivered by the determinate counsel and foreknowledge of God, ye have taken, and by wicked hands have crucified and slain: Whom God hath raised up, having loosed the pains of death: because it was not possible that he should be holden of it.*

For David speaketh concerning him, I foresaw the Lord always before my face, for he is on my right hand, that I should not be moved: Therefore did my heart rejoice, and my tongue was glad; moreover also my flesh shall rest in hope: Because thou wilt not leave my soul in hell, neither wilt thou suffer thine Holy One to see corruption.

Thou hast made known to me the ways of life; thou shalt make me full of joy with thy countenance.

Men and brethren, let me freely speak unto you of the patriarch David, that he is both dead and buried, and his sepulchre is with us unto this day.

Therefore being a prophet, and knowing that God had sworn with an oath to him, that of the fruit of his loins, according to the flesh, he would raise up Christ to sit on his throne; **He seeing this before spake of the resurrection of Christ, that his soul was not left in hell, neither his flesh did see corruption.**

This Jesus hath God raised up, whereof we all are witnesses.

Therefore being by the right hand of God exalted, and having received of the Father the promise of the Holy Ghost, he hath shed forth this, which ye now see and hear.

For David is not ascended into the heavens: but he saith himself, The LORD said unto my Lord, Sit thou on my right hand, Until I make thy foes thy footstool.

Therefore let all the house of Israel know assuredly, that God hath made that same Jesus, whom ye have crucified, both Lord and Christ."

(ACTS 2:22–36)

And so Jesus went into hell to face the powers of darkness and to defeat all of the demons of hell to give us authority against them. That is what Paul is talking about in this next scripture;

"Blotting out the handwriting of ordinances that was against us, which was contrary to us, and took it out of the way, nailing it to his cross; **and having spoiled principalities and powers, he made a shew of them openly, triumphing over them in it.***"*

(COLOSSIANS 2:14–15)

That is why we can cast out demons today, since it had never been done in the Old Testament before! None of the saints under the Old Covenant had the authority to cast out devils until Jesus came onto the scene. Jesus came to establish the ministry of deliverance which started with His own ministry (which only lasted a short season of around three and a half years until the cross). And we are now in a long season of two thousand years of the church with signs and wonders as a result of what Jesus did. Hallelujah!

Sometimes it only takes a short season to ignite a much longer season! Remember that it took Jesus three days to conquer Satan and all of his demons which gave us over two thousand years of victory over him. But without that three days of Jesus being separated from His Father we would not have had the church at all.

Some seasons are very hard to understand. I still find it hard to understand why the children of Israel were held captive for four hundred and thirty years until freedom came. Was it because God could not find a man that He could fully trust? Maybe that is it?

Moses had to go through all kinds of seasons until he was ready to take on Egypt. As he entered the scene there had been a long season of four hundred and thirty years which did not look as if it would ever change. Then Moses was given a mandate from the Lord at the burning bush to deliver God's people from slavery. In the book of Exodus we have the amazing account of Moses confronting Pharaoh many times to let His people go. It was a relatively short season of signs and wonders before he finally gave in when the destroyer came and took all of the firstborn in Egypt.

This brought about a completely new season in the history of Israel. Just one man who believes and obeys God can make such a tremendous change in the lives of millions of people.

Sometimes God calls us to a short season which we don't particularly enjoy, but it has a profound impact on our life and those we influence.

That is why it is imperative that we obey His voice when He speaks to us. As the people of God we are His servants and thus should be willing to do whatever He tells us to do. It can have an amazing impact on the kingdom of God when we do what the Father says. Just do it! Like the Nike advert!

I am just thinking about some of the natural seasons of life. A woman who has children probably does not think that she has an enormous responsibility for about a third of her life until her children are grown up. Also, when we start our career it takes up over half of our entire life while we are in that season. Most people work for forty years, some a few more and some less, but that is one of the longest seasons in our life. That is why it is important for you to find the right job, because you are going to be doing it for a very long time! Eight hours a day, five days a week, for the next forty years! I believe that God has the right job for all of His children, where they can be satisfied with their work and have the chance to witness about Jesus Christ and make a good living for their family. We each have different talents and abilities that can be used in this world to good effect. As you seek God He will show you what you are to do with your life and career.

It is a very big season and so it is one that you need to get right. God has a job waiting with your name on it.

CHAPTER 6

A SEASON OF WEEPING

"For his anger endureth but a moment; in his favour is life: **weeping may endure for a night, but joy cometh in the morning.**"

(PSALM 30:5)

"Blessed are they that dwell in thy house: they will be still praising thee. Selah. Blessed is the man whose strength is in thee; in whose heart are the ways of them. **Who passing through the valley of Baca make it a well**; *the rain also filleth the pools. They go from strength to strength, every one of them in Zion appeareth before God."*

(PSALM 84:4–7)

"So Hannah rose up after they had eaten in Shiloh, and after they had drunk. Now Eli the priest sat upon a seat by a post of the temple of the LORD. **And she was in bitterness of soul, and prayed unto the** LORD, **and wept sore.** *And she vowed a vow, and said, O* LORD *of hosts, if thou wilt indeed look on the affliction of thine handmaid, and remember me, and not forget thine handmaid, but wilt give unto thine handmaid a man child, then I will give him unto the* LORD *all the days of his life, and there shall no razor come upon his head."*

(1 SAMUEL 1:9–11)

"Thou tellest my wanderings: **put thou my tears into thy bottle:** *are they not in thy book?"*

(PSALM 56:8)

In Psalm 84 above it mentions the valley of Baca. It can equally be translated as "the valley of weeping". Notice it says that we *pass through* Baca. We are not meant to spend the rest of our lives weeping, but to simply pass through as a season. You will also see that having passed through the valley of weeping, they went "from strength to strength". So we are to grow in strength whenever we go through a season of weeping. Hannah cried out so strongly to God that He heard her cry and gave her a son!

I like that verse above about God keeping all of our tears in His bottle. There is a big one with my name on it that is for sure! I have shed my fair share of tears over the years.

I went through a season of weeping many years ago when we were young and the children were small. We were trusting the Lord for all of our food every day. The thought of buying clothes was an impossible one, since we did not even have enough income to pay our basic bills.

Each night Ruth and I would go to bed and I would look at her clothes which were threadbare and looked most of the time as if holes would appear. She never complained at all to me, even though she was used to having nice things when she was a girl. When Ruth was asleep I would quietly cry myself to sleep since I felt responsible for not being able to provide for my wife. I did this for years each night, but since Ruth falls asleep very quickly she never saw me. I could not see an end to that season since we were always believing God for our basic needs such as food and domestic bills. I was often sent to churches where there was very little and had to build them up. As soon as I was earning a proper wage I was sent again to another struggling church to build that one up. Looking back I can see that it was the best experience for an apostle, which is what the Lord was preparing me for, even though I had no idea at the time.

It was a season of weeping regarding natural things and I am glad to report that I do not weep any more since I am able to buy Ruth nice clothes these days! It is a joy to be able to give her some money every so often and tell her to go and spend it on herself. Ruth is so precious and not materialistic at all and so I have to force her to go shopping!

Most people go through things that cause a season of weeping. Maybe you are in such a season right now. It will come to an end! Joy is around the corner! Hannah wept bitterly but her baby came along.

"Then shall the virgin rejoice in the dance, both young men and old together: for I will turn their mourning into joy, and will comfort them, and make them rejoice from their sorrow."

(JEREMIAH 31:13)

"In his neck remaineth strength, and sorrow is turned into joy before him."

(JOB 41:22)

"Verily, verily, I say unto you, That ye shall weep and lament, but the world shall rejoice: and ye shall be sorrowful, but your sorrow shall be turned into joy."

(JOHN 16:20)

We are also commanded to bring comfort to those who weep.

"Rejoice with them that do rejoice, and weep with them that weep."

(ROMANS 12:15)

Tears are supposed to be very good for the skin also!

Some people actually cry during a session of deliverance which is interesting. That does not mean that you are being delivered from something each time you cry!

Many have testified to feeling much better after they have wept. It seems to be a natural way of letting something out. I have often wept when I read the Word of God as His Presence overwhelms me. I regularly weep during worship as the manifest presence of God comes upon me.

All seasons come to an end, including weeping. Pass through the valley of Baca and don't make your home there! Joy and victory are waiting for you also! A new season of breakthrough and victory usually comes after such a season and the Lord always draws particularly close during this time.

> *"Hear, O LORD, and have mercy upon me: LORD, be thou my helper. Thou hast turned for me my mourning into dancing: thou hast put off my sackcloth, and girded me with gladness; To the end that my glory may sing praise to thee, and not be silent. O LORD my God, I will give thanks unto thee for ever."*
>
> (PSALM 30:10–12)

The Lord has some very creative ways to turn our situations around and bring glory out of awful circumstances. I personally think that God enjoys a challenge and loves to show Himself in situations that we consider to be impossible.

> *"And Jesus looking upon them saith, With men it is impossible, but not with God: for with God all things are possible."*
>
> (MARK 10:27)

> *"For with God nothing shall be impossible."*
>
> (LUKE 1:37)

> *"But without faith it is impossible to please him: for he that cometh to God must believe that he is, and that he is a rewarder of them that diligently seek him."*
>
> (HEBREWS 11:6)

Thus we need to have faith in our season of weeping and expect God to turn our captivity around for His glory, our victory, and the devil's embarrassment!

CHAPTER 7

A SEASON OF STUDY AND PREPARATION

I went through a season many years ago when I first entered Christian ministry which was an essential time in my life. I found myself pastoring a small church in Garston, Liverpool. There were only about ten people in the church and I was the pastor. I had not been to Bible College but had wanted to go and study for ministry. However, the Lord had different plans for me. I came under my dear pastor Aubrey Whittall from the Liverpool church who became my mentor. He helped me considerably in my early years and I was always asking him questions about doctrine or ministerial practice. He had been in ministry for decades and knew the Scriptures so well.

After I had been leading the church for a few months and was intending to go to Bible College, the Lord began to speak to me and told me clearly not to go. I could not understand this. Wasn't everyone supposed to go for training before leading a church? I really struggled with this word from God for months, but in the end I told Him that I would do what He said to me. I wrote to the principal of the Bible College and he told me that I had two other choices I could pursue on my own if I was not going to study at the College itself. I opted to do twelve theses on the twelve fundamental beliefs of the Pentecostal ministry. I really enjoyed it and studied for hours each day. It was a season of study that has prepared me for a lifetime of ministering God's Word all over the world. I never knew when I was sitting in that small bedroom in Speke, Liverpool, that I would one day be flying around the world and speaking at churches and conferences in so many countries.

Now I realise that I could never be doing what I am doing today without those years of intense study. It was the best preparation that I could have had. I wanted a season at the College, but God wanted me to have a season in a bedroom with His Word and few concordances.

There are times when I am preaching today when things will come out of me that I studied all those years ago. It is in me because of that season.

That season lasted for about two years. I studied for between eight and thirteen hours a day for four days a week. The other day during the week I spent visiting and then there was the weekend. Thus a two year season prepared me for the next fifty years of ministry!

Ruth and I then left Liverpool to go to Salford in Manchester where we took over another church that was struggling. A new season started in my life in more ways than one. It was in Salford that I learned how to be an intercessor. I spoke in tongues, but I had never developed any more than that. My pastor had often told me about the languages of the Spirit, but I had been so busy studying that I had not really had the opportunity to grow in this area. So I made some time each day and prayed in the Holy Spirit. It was hard at first, but I was determined to break through. I started with just twenty minutes the first day and then twenty-three minutes the next day. After a week I was praying in tongues for over an hour; then two hours, and so on. I knew that I was breaking through into a new realm of spiritual growth. Ruth used to listen in to me praying and said that I was mad!

I knew that things were happening as new languages kept coming out of me. I did this for two years. During this season of prayer I experienced some amazing results in the church. The gifts of the Spirit started to break out on Sundays. Miracles started to happen each Sunday during the meetings and I knew that it was direct result of seeking God in intercession. I changed so much during this time and grew closer to God.

Ruth saw the change in me and told me that she was going to start to pray in the Spirit each night while I was out at meetings. She would try and not much happened. When I arrived home she would say to me that nothing was happening. I told her to keep doing it until she got a breakthrough. It took many months, but Ruth broke through also. Our lives changed so much and it affected our ministry so much. I even wrote a booklet called *How to Pray in the Spirit* which is still in print if you want to order a copy.

When I first began in ministry I made a decision right at the start that I would fast regularly each week. During the first fourteen years of ministry I fasted at least two days per week, sometimes three days. I drank much water during fasting, which is wise since there is a lot of water in food. This season helped me much to grow close to the Lord and to prepare me for a worldwide ministry.

When I started travelling internationally I realised that it was difficult to fast when speaking so much, and so I changed the way I fasted. Instead of fasting each week for a few days I began another season of long fasts. I had never fasted longer than four days since I was fasting every week. So I did my first seven day fast. Then I did ten days. After a while I did a fourteen day fast. I found that after the first three days my stomach settled down and did not expect food, so the next ten days were quite easy. The first three or four days seem to be the worst.

When I was thirty-nine I developed a pain in my side that I rebuked and took authority against. It did not go away even though I did everything that I knew to do. So I prayed in the Spirit until God spoke to my heart. He told me to fast for longer than I had done before. I had done a fourteen day fast already, so I decided to fast for twenty-one days with no food at all. I looked at my diary and booked the fast when my schedule was at a minimum. I only preached six times during that fast. I got to ten days and the pain was still there; fourteen days and I was still in pain, just like before; sixteen days and still in pain. I kept confessing the Word of

God over my body. On day seventeen in the evening I heard a small "pop" sound from my side and felt something leave me. I was healed from that day forward. That was seven years ago and it has not returned.

The Scriptures teach that fasting speeds up the healing process.

> "**Is not this the fast that I have chosen**? *to loose the bands of wickedness, to undo the heavy burdens, and to let the oppressed go free, and that ye break every yoke?*
>
> *Is it not to deal thy bread to the hungry, and that thou bring the poor that are cast out to thy house? when thou seest the naked, that thou cover him; and that thou hide not thyself from thine own flesh?*
>
> *Then shall thy light break forth as the morning,* **and thine health shall spring forth speedily**: *and thy righteousness shall go before thee; the glory of the* LORD *shall be thy reward."*
>
> (ISAIAH 58:6–8)

I have used this method of healing a few times now and it works to the glory of God.

So I started with a season of study, then moved to a season of prayer, during which time I was fasting regularly. Then another season began!

I always knew that God had a wider ministry for me and that my time in the Elim Pentecostal Church would only be for a season. It came to an end in 1989 and we moved back to Stoke on Trent. I knew that a new season of ministry was ahead of me, but I did not know what to do. So we sat under Philip Parsons' ministry for six months and spent time listening to the Holy Spirit. I was working for a short season as a financial advisor with Royal Insurance, but I knew that God was doing a work in my heart. I used to spend one day each week in prayer and would walk for miles just praying and seeking God for the next step in my life. One day God spoke to me so clearly and told me to go to the Saltbox and book a room and hold some teaching meetings. I contacted Lloyd Cooke and he said to me, "What are you going to call yourselves?" It was a good question to which I did not know the answer. He went away and played on his computer and came back and said, "What about 'Life Changing Ministries'?" I told him that it sounded OK and so we launched LCM with a weekly meeting at the Saltbox in Burslem, Stoke on Trent.

That was fourteen years ago. We had no money, no people, no equipment, no musicians and no support from anyone. Just a word from God in my heart. Today LCM has touched people all over the world. Our books alone have been read by people in at least one hundred and twenty countries that we know about. We currently have over three hundred churches that look to us for apostolic covering. We also have our own weekly TV programme that reaches potentially millions around the UK and Europe. Despise not the day of small beginnings! When I obeyed the Lord just fourteen years ago, I could never have dreamed that I would preach the gospel in sixty countries of the world to thousands at a time. I am shortly to speak to a conference in South Korea with five thousand people with me as the main speaker. I never thought that I would get to speak to so many people. God takes us on one step at a time and through many seasons to prepare us for our destiny.

CHAPTER 8

A Season
of Battles
and Trials

I am sure that many of you can already identify with this chapter title without even starting to read the chapter!

As a pioneer I am often involved in breaking new ground and getting things started. I love the challenge of bringing something out of nothing! However, you have to be ready for all kinds of battles and trials. Let us see what the Word of God says:

"How that in a great trial of affliction the abundance of their joy and their deep poverty abounded unto the riches of their liberality."

(2 CORINTHIANS 8:2)

"Wherein ye greatly rejoice, though now for a season, if need be, ye are in heaviness through manifold temptations: That the trial of your faith, being much more precious than of gold that perisheth, though it be tried with fire, might be found unto praise and honour and glory at the appearing of Jesus Christ *Whom having not seen, ye love; in whom, though now ye see him not, yet believing, ye rejoice with joy unspeakable and full of glory: Receiving the end of your faith, even the salvation of your souls."*

(1 PETER 1:6–9)

"Beloved, think it not strange concerning the fiery trial which is to try you, as though some strange thing happened unto you: But rejoice, inasmuch as ye are partakers of Christ's sufferings; that, when his glory shall be revealed, ye may be glad also with exceeding joy.

If ye be reproached for the name of Christ, happy are ye; for the spirit of glory and of God resteth upon you: on their part he is evil spoken of, but on your part he is glorified."

(1 PETER 4:12–14)

All sorts of persecution can come upon us simply for being Christians even without starting a new church!

"Yea, and all that will live godly in Christ Jesus shall suffer persecution."

(2 Timothy 3:12)

Therefore, if you are leading a godly life then you are promised some persecution for your faith. The secret is to rejoice in such persecution. Ruth and I have had to rejoice a lot over the last fourteen years since we have had so many attacks against us.

For the first few years of LCM it seemed like we were in a constant season of one attack after another. One would finish and another would start. This season lasted for about nine years. All I was doing was obeying God and all hell was let loose on us! I realised that we were simply invading the devil's kingdom and that he wanted us to quit before we became established. The devil does not wait until you are established before he attacks you. Many people fold in under the pressure and abort God's will. That is the devil's plan to stop God's work from prospering. We have had so many awkward people that we have tried to love and support and they have turned around and tried to destroy us! I have had to walk in much forgiveness and love and simply give such people over to the Lord and let Him deal with them. I admit that it has been very difficult at times and I have been severely tempted to give it all up and have a quiet life as a salesman! I saw a job one time that the devil tempted me with. I was on holiday and going through a really hard time with grumblers and complainers moaning and groaning about this and that. I looked at the job and the devil said to me, "You could get that job easily." I thought to myself, "Yes, I could." The job had a starting salary of

£50,000 a year rising to £75,000 after six months with a brand new Mercedes Benz each year. I almost made that call and knew that I could get the job and do the ministry part time. This season went on for about two years with severe temptations to take a job and stop trusting God for the finances. Every day I would wake up and Satan would speak to my heart and tell me that it was not worth all of the hassle and that I should get a job that pays proper money.

I resisted him because I knew that it was the devil's voice. I did not want to give him any victory at all. If I had taken a job I could not have done any of the work that the Lord has called me to. No books, no churches abroad, no TV ministry etc. There is a principle here. When you are in the perfect centre of the will of God then Satan will try and get you doing something else. You have to fight to stay in the will of God.

I am so glad that I kept going through so many trials of faith. We had people who would say such terrible things about us that were just not true. The devil must have known something about how LCM was going to influence so many for righteousness. I get letters every week from all over the world about our books being used to train leaders in Bible Colleges, Bible studies, house groups and churches. It is amazing to see so much fruit. I could never have believed that God was going to do so much. I just sit back and laugh sometimes and worship the Lord who has brought us through so much hardship. He is an awesome God and I love Him more now than ever.

One thing that I have learned through all of these trials and afflictions and that is God is refining us and shaping us for His glory.

"But he knoweth the way that I take: **when he hath tried me, I shall come forth as gold."**

(JOB 23:10)

"And I will bring the third part through the fire, and will refine them as silver is refined, and will try them as gold is tried: they shall call on my name, and I will hear them: I will say, It is my people: and they shall say, The LORD is my God."

(ZECHARIAH 13:9)

If ever you find yourself having to deal with somebody that is so difficult and awkward it could be that God has put them there to rub some rough edges off you! We always want to be with people that agree with us all the time, but you do not grow in the fruit of the Spirit by having to deal with those who only agree all the time. It is those people you meet who seem to misunderstand you constantly that you can learn from. That is why God often brings people together who are opposites in marriage! We can learn from each other. I have learnt so much from being married to Ruth and we have helped each other to grow in grace so much after twenty-four years! We are so much in love these days as we have got closer to each other.

I am glad to report that such trials are only for a season! Hallelujah! There was a time when I did not think that it would ever end, but it has. I have such peace these days in our church. That season is over! It has prepared me for the next season in my life.

CHAPTER 9

THE SEASONS OF PATIENCE

Let us take a look at what God's Word says regarding patience.

> *"And not only so, but we glory in tribulations also: knowing that tribulation worketh patience; and patience, experience; and experience, hope."*
>
> (ROMANS 5:3–4)

> *"But if we hope for that we see not, then do we with patience wait for it."*
>
> (ROMANS 8:25)

"For whatsoever things were written aforetime were written for our learning, that we through patience and comfort of the scriptures might have hope. Now the God of patience and consolation grant you to be likeminded one toward another according to Christ Jesus."

(ROMANS 15:4–5)

"But in all things approving ourselves as the ministers of God, in much patience, in afflictions, in necessities, in distresses."

(2 CORINTHIANS 6:4)

"Truly the signs of an apostle were wrought among you in all patience, in signs, and wonders, and mighty deeds."

(2 CORINTHIANS 12:12)

"Strengthened with all might, according to his glorious power, unto all patience and longsuffering with joyfulness."

(COLOSSIANS 1:11)

"For ye have need of patience, that, after ye have done the will of God, ye might receive the promise."

(HEBREWS 10:36)

"Wherefore seeing we also are compassed about with so great a cloud of witnesses, let us lay aside every weight, and the sin which doth so easily beset us, and let us run with patience the race that is set before us."

(HEBREWS 12:1)

"Knowing this, that the trying of your faith worketh patience. But let patience have her perfect work, that ye may be perfect and entire, wanting nothing."

(JAMES 1:3–4)

"Be patient therefore, brethren, unto the coming of the Lord. Behold, the husbandman waiteth for the precious fruit of the earth, and hath long patience for it, until he receive the early and latter rain."

(JAMES 5:7)

I don't think that anybody likes patience. Why can't I have it now! We all have to learn the patience lesson if we are to achieve the high call of God upon our lives. I watch people regularly who are very anxious to do things in the kingdom, but I see things in them that would mar so much good if they were to be given too much too soon. If I can see those things, then how much more can God see them? Now I know that God does not wait until we are perfect before He uses us, or else nobody would ever do anything in the kingdom! But there are some things that just have to be sorted out and that takes time, which means patience. Take a look at the following list and see if any of these things register in your heart.

1. Pride. God resists the proud but gives grace to the humble (see James 4:6).
2. Arrogance.
3. Ego and selfish ambition.
4. A haughty spirit.
5. Selfishness.

6. Bad attitudes towards others when they are promoted.
7. Jealousy and envy.
8. Impure motives.
9. Rashness.
10. Holding grudges.
11. Looking down on others.
12. Anything else?
    (Write it here: . . . .)

If God has spoken to you about how He is going to use you then it will take time before it all works out. The Lord wants clean and pure people to do His work in every area of life. The refining season is one to be taken seriously. Take a look at this verse which has always challenged me:

"I the LORD search the heart, I try the reins, even to give every man according to his ways, and according to the fruit of his doings."

(JEREMIAH 17:10)

The heart here can be translated as "feelings, the will and the intellect, the centre of everything". The reins can be translated as "the mind". And ways can be translated as "course of life or mode of action".

Thus God is watching us all the time to see how we do things. He is examining our heart in each thing that we do to see if we are ready to do His will. I have often been aware of the Lord watching over me and it is as if He is assessing me when I do certain things. This is all to do with the patience process. If you are found to be impatient and try to rush things on a bit you will stumble and fall. The Lord will show you when He is ready to move you on – in His way and in His time.

Study this verse over and over again until you get some revelation on it!

> "**My times are in thy hand**: *deliver me from the hand of mine enemies, and from them that persecute me.*"
>
> (PSALM 31:15)

The word "times" above can equally be translated seasons: "**My seasons are in thy hand.**"

God cannot bring you up higher until you have learned your lessons in your current season. You have to learn to rejoice in your present season and say, "I am patient Lord for I know that You have my life in Your hands."

> "*For promotion cometh neither from the east, nor from the west, nor from the south. But God is the judge: he putteth down one, and setteth up another.*"
>
> (PSALM 75:6–7)

You have to become patient with God and those who are your leaders. They have an awesome responsibility to help you in your development. You need to trust their decisions as ones who must give an account to God about you.

Some prayers take time to be answered which requires patience. I have been a Christian now for twenty-seven years and I am still waiting for my parents to come to Christ. Now that takes patience! I have felt like shouting at them or shaking them to wake up out of their complacency. I know that I have to be patient and trust God to visit their hearts by His Spirit. I have done all that I can do, now God will do what I cannot do!

Another area of patience is when the Lord speaks to you about you doing something for Him. I was twenty-four years old when the Lord said to me that one day I would preach the gospel on British TV every week. When God said that to me it was actually impossible to do that in Britain. I waited patiently over the years and wondered if it would ever come to pass. It was around 1999 that the law in the UK changed and Christian TV became a reality. Straight away we started to support the God Channel each month as a seed, as well as to help them reach our generation. Now we have our own TV studio, camera team and weekly programme after twenty-one years of patient waiting.

Everything that God says to you will come to pass if you wait patiently for Him. You need a revelation of patience.

One lady came to her pastor and said to him. "Pastor please pray for me to have patience." He thought for a bit and then prayed this over her, "Lord bring every possible trial and temptation to this lady so that she learns your patience!" She was shocked, but the pastor was right. It takes time to learn patience God's way. The sooner you grow up in patience the sooner you will realise your dreams!

The season of patience is often one of the toughest lessons to learn, but learn it we must!

CHAPTER 10

A SEASON ON DEATH ROW!

I recently received a letter from Africa from a man who had just read one of my books whilst in prison. He was requesting more books to help him to grow spiritually. I sent him some and he was very grateful.

I don't know why he finds himself in the maximum security section on death row. He did not tell me. I can only assume that he committed a very serious offence and then found Jesus Christ in prison. But he finds himself in a season that few Christians will ever have to go through. We don't know how long he will have before he is executed for his crime. I assume that he does not know either. He simply has to wait in his cell for the day of execution. What a season that is. I am quite sure that he has repented many times and asked God for forgiveness. His letters do seem to show a real depth of relationship with God. In the natural way this will be his last season on earth at just thirty-seven years old. He told me about his wife and child who he does not see. All he has is the Lord.

I wonder what you and I would be like if ever we found ourselves in such a situation. It is hard to imagine what it must be like. Perhaps he is even praying for his execution to come quickly so that he can enjoy heaven sooner? Maybe he is trusting and believing for a reprieve or even a miracle to be released?

When we compare some of our seasons to the plight of this young man it can help us to put things into perspective. Paul the apostle went through all kinds of horrible seasons and yet he says this:

> *"For all things are for your sakes, that the abundant grace might through the thanksgiving of many redound to the glory of God. For which cause we faint not; but though our outward man perish, yet the inward man is renewed day by day. **For our light affliction, which is but for a moment**, worketh for us a far more exceeding and eternal weight of glory. While we look not at the things which are seen, but at the things which are not seen: for the things which are seen are temporal; but the things which are not seen are eternal."*

(2 CORINTHIANS 4:15–18)

Let us look at some of Paul's seasons of afflictions:

"Are they ministers of Christ? (I speak as a fool) I am more; in labours more abundant, in stripes above measure, in prisons more frequent, in deaths oft. Of the Jews five times received I forty stripes save one. Thrice was I beaten with rods, once was I stoned, thrice I suffered shipwreck, a night and a day I have been in the deep; In journeyings often, in perils of waters, in perils of robbers, in perils by mine own countrymen, in perils by the heathen, in perils in the city, in perils in the wilderness, in perils in the sea, in perils among false brethren; In weariness and painfulness, in watchings often, in hunger and thirst, in fastings often, in cold and nakedness. Beside those things that are without, that which cometh upon me daily, the care of all the churches. Who is weak, and I am not weak? who is offended, and I burn not?"

(2 CORINTHIANS 11:23–29)

And yet Paul says "our light afflictions"! That was how Paul saw his own afflictions in the light of eternity! It does take some faith when you are in the middle of a trying season, but if you can stop and think about the duration of your season compared to the eternal ages, as Paul did, then it can help you to rejoice in any situation.

I remember a story a few years ago that caused me to weep. A young pastor who had several children was told by his government to stop preaching the gospel in public. He continued and was unmoved by the threat. They gave him one more chance to stop, but he just kept on preaching about Jesus and so they put him into prison. They decided to inflict a horrible means of torture on him by immersing him in human excrement up to his chin for eighteen hours a day. All for declaring the precious gospel. He started to complain to the Lord and asked Him why this was happening. The Lord spoke to him clearly and said to him that if he could learn to rejoice in that situation then he could rejoice in any situation! He started to put on the garments of praise instead of moaning and that season came to an abrupt end. He was released with no charge in a few days and not told why.

That story has always stuck with me. We need to learn to rejoice in whatever season we find ourselves in and not to question God at all.

> *"Not that I speak in respect of want: for I have learned, in whatsoever state I am, therewith to be content. I know both how to be abased, and I know how to abound: every where and in all things I am instructed both to be full and to be hungry, both to abound and to suffer need. I can do all things through Christ which strengtheneth me."*
>
> (PHILIPPIANS 4:11–13)

I think that it helps us to remember those who are in real adversity and to see that we are going through little compared to some folk.

CHAPTER 11

A LONG SEASON INDEED

I had the pleasure many years ago to meet an old frail couple who told me their story. When they were just twenty-one years old they felt strongly that God had called them to go onto the mission field. They took this calling very seriously and started to apply to different missionary organisations. They were refused by all of them, but they kept trying for quite a lengthy season. After many refusals they both decided that their efforts were in vain, so they began praying for direction from the Lord as to what they should do.

After some time in prayer they both felt that they should simply go by faith to an un-evangelised country. They sailed all the way to Papua New Guinea. They had no money or promise of support from anybody. They went on a word from God to their hearts. They learned the language and adapted to the local way of life. They built a mud hut, ate the same food as the locals and mixed with the people of Papua New Guinea. As bright young people they were able to learn the language quickly and to speak to the people about Jesus Christ and His love. Nobody responded. The months turned into years and nobody accepted Christ Jesus. Ten years passed and still not one convert. They were determined to carry on. They kept praying and witnessing to the people for another decade and still nobody came to Christ. Phew! What a season! I wonder how many people would have carried on after twenty years without a single convert!

Their health suffered many times through poor nutrition. But they kept going for the sake of a country who did not know Jesus Christ at all.

After thirty years they had still not seen any converts but kept going! Now that is a long season without any fruit for their labour. But we cannot see what is going on behind the scenes in the spiritual realm as a result of our work.

It took another five years before they saw any fruit. All of a sudden people started to get saved and come to Christ. Their patience was paying off at long last.

Could you have gone on for thirty-five years without any results? I don't think that I could at all. That couple have inspired me tremendously to keep going even when the going gets tough.

Hundreds and thousands have since come to know Jesus Christ in Papua New Guinea as a result of that precious couple. They are now sending out missionaries all over the country and even into other countries!

What a season! What patience! What determination and diligence!

The devil is an aborter of God's plans. His job is to try to stop us fulfilling the Father's plans on this earth. That is often why we go through seasons of opposition, trials, temptations, awkward people etc. Satan wants us to quit!

> *"And let us not be weary in well doing: for in due season we shall reap, if we faint not."*
>
> (GALATIANS 6:9)

> *"But ye, brethren, be not weary in well doing."*
>
> (2 THESSALONIANS 3:13)

The missionary couple had that revelation! They just kept going and believing that one day God would pour out His Spirit upon the seeds they had planted. That story motivates me so much. I pray that it encourages you in whatever season you find yourself in.

CHAPTER 12

A SEASON OF SOWING

Let us take a look at some scriptures:

> *"Hearken; Behold, there went out a sower to sow: And it came to pass, as he sowed, some fell by the way side, and the fowls of the air came and devoured it up.*
>
> *And some fell on stony ground, where it had not much earth; and immediately it sprang up, because it had no depth of earth: But when the sun was up, it was scorched; and because it had no root, it withered away.*
>
> *And some fell among thorns, and the thorns grew up, and choked it, and it yielded no fruit.*

And other fell on good ground, and did yield fruit that sprang up and increased; and brought forth, some thirty, and some sixty, and some an hundred.

And he said unto them, He that hath ears to hear, let him hear.

And when he was alone, they that were about him with the twelve asked of him the parable.

And he said unto them, Unto you it is given to know the mystery of the kingdom of God: but unto them that are without, all these things are done in parables: That seeing they may see, and not perceive; and hearing they may hear, and not understand; lest at any time they should be converted, and their sins should be forgiven them.

And he said unto them, Know ye not this parable? and how then will ye know all parables?

The sower soweth the word.

And these are they by the way side, where the word is sown; but when they have heard, Satan cometh immediately, and taketh away the word that was sown in their hearts.

And these are they likewise which are sown on stony ground; who, when they have heard the word, immediately receive it with gladness; And have no root in themselves, and so endure but for a time: afterward, when affliction or persecution ariseth for the word's sake, immediately they are offended.

And these are they which are sown among thorns; such as hear the word, And the cares of this world, and the deceitfulness of riches, and the lusts of other things entering in, choke the word, and it becometh unfruitful.

And these are they which are sown on good ground; such as hear the word, and receive it, and bring forth fruit, some thirtyfold, some sixty, and some an hundred."

(MARK 4:3–20)

So according to these words of Jesus you are always going to come under attack when you start to sow your seeds. Whatever kind of seed you are sowing in the kingdom of God, the devil will oppose you. You have to learn to stand firm and resist the devil from your mind mostly. Have you ever heard these words in your mind: "Nothing is happening to your seeds, why bother doing it at all"? Remember that the devil is liar and so if he says to you that something is not working, then you obviously know that it is working! He cannot tell the truth since he is a consistent liar. If the devil says to you that you are going to die, then you will live. If he says that you will never get healed, then you are going to be healed.

Take a careful look at what Jesus said about the devil:

"Ye are of your father the devil, and the lusts of your father ye will do. **He was a murderer from the beginning, and abode not in the truth, because there is no truth in him.** *When he speaketh a lie, he speaketh of his own: for he is a liar, and the father of it."*

(JOHN 8:44)

That is such a revelation. God cannot lie and the devil cannot tell the truth! They are both consistent!

So why do you listen to the devil's lies and believe them? Particularly when you are going through a challenging season in your life the devil will try and tell you all sorts of lies. It is his usual tactic and we need to learn it if we are to live in victory.

Jesus told us in the parable of the sower that the thief would try to come and steal the seed that was sown. He does not wait until it has taken root, but strikes straight away. Whenever you sow any type of seed you need to be on your guard against the enemy that he does not try one of his usual tricks to rob you of blessing.

If you want a season of harvest in your life then you will have to have a season of sowing. It is spiritual law. You can't have a harvest without sowing seed first.

So many people in the kingdom have missed this. They are asking God to do things for them without ever sowing any seed. Get your seeds into the ground first and be patient for your harvest.

In our current ministry we have been sowing seeds for nearly fifteen years – seeds of prayer, evangelism, finances and time. For many years we saw nothing, but I knew that we were in the will of God. That is important to establish first before you do any seed sowing. Are you in the will of God? I spent six months seeking the Lord until I had heard clearly from Him before we did anything. Once He spoke to me I knew that He would anoint the work of my hands as I stayed in His will. Every few months I used to go away and seek God's face to make sure that I was staying in His will at all times. They were mini seasons of prayer and God would always speak to me about the next step for Life Changing Ministries.

It took about eleven years until we started to see some major breakthroughs in our ministry. We stood in faith for those eleven years believing what He had said. Things looked very slow, but in the last three years we have seen so many breakthroughs. The season of sowing has turned into a season of harvest! Hallelujah! Keep on doing what you are doing in the will of God and it will happen.

"If thou wouldest seek unto God betimes, and make thy supplication to the Almighty; If thou wert pure and upright; surely now he would awake for thee, and make the habitation of thy righteousness prosperous. **Though thy beginning was small, yet thy latter end should greatly increase.***"*

(JOB 8:5–7)

I used to stand on this verse regularly in our season of faith and I can honestly say that it is coming to pass. From such humble beginnings in our lounge with just six people LCM has become a global ministry. I have recently been on one of the major secular TV channels to minister deliverance to over two million people in one night.

We simply need to be faithful in the little that we are doing today and the Lord will breathe on what you are doing and bring you into a new season of blessing.

"His lord said unto him, **Well done, good and faithful servant; thou hast been faithful over a few things, I will make thee ruler over many things***: enter thou into the joy of thy lord."*

(MATTHEW 25:23)

Our seasons are in His hands! We cannot force the next season. It is the Lord that opens doors that no man can shut.

"And to the angel of the church in Philadelphia write; **These things saith he that is holy, he that is true, he that hath the key of David, he that openeth, and no man shutteth; and shutteth, and no man openeth***."*

(REVELATION 3:7)

This is where patience is needed in your present season. If you will wait for His time then you will see the glory of God. One thing about patience that some people miss is that we need to be patient joyfully and not grudgingly! Some get frustrated and angry during the sowing season and even become bitter towards God because nothing appears to be happening. God can change things in an instant! I have seen Him do it for both myself and others. Impatient people never find the high calling of God for their life. It is a vital ingredient.

Keep sowing good seed into good ground and watch your heart with all diligence and your day will come.

> *"Keep thy heart with all diligence; for out of it are the issues of life. Put away from thee a froward mouth, and perverse lips put far from thee. Let thine eyes look right on, and let thine eyelids look straight before thee. Ponder the path of thy feet, and let all thy ways be established. Turn not to the right hand nor to the left: remove thy foot from evil."*
>
> (PROVERBS 4:23–27)

CHAPTER 13

TWO UNEXPECTED SEASONS

I am currently in two seasons that completely took me by surprise when they started. I told the Lord many years ago that I hated writing, since I failed English Language three times at school. Consequently I never wanted to write a book. Also, I never wanted to travel abroad!

The year was 1992 and I was busy helping to get our church established. The last thing on my mind was either writing a book or travelling overseas. But I was fasting and praying one day and God spoke to me very clearly saying, "Write a book." I was shocked for days and told the Lord how much I did not want to do it, but that I would just because He had said it. I began writing my first book and spent six months writing every day, only managing twenty-four pages! It was so hard. We got it published and I thought that that would be the end of writing for me. Then the Lord told me to write a large book. So I obeyed and it took me so long to do all that work. Also, I had no idea about how we could possibly pay for it. It cost over £4,000 to produce. The manuscript lay on my desk for eighteen months as I believed God for the money. One day a kind gentleman said that he would give me £250 towards the book which was such a blessing. A few months later we published *The Ministry of Jesus Christ* with New Wine Press.

Again I did not expect to do any more writing, but God spoke to me again and so I obeyed Him once more and stood in faith for the money. I have now written twenty books and the time that it now takes me to write a larger book is about four days. God has given me such a love for writing, even though I hated it to start with. I am a mathematician and I love to find the shortest method to do any job. People say that my books are easy to read since I get straight to the point! Some writers woffle for page after page before they say anything!

I thought that my writing season would be short, but it has gone on for thirteen years with no sign of stopping. I have another three books growing inside me right now.

The other total surprise was international travelling. I did not have a passport until I was thirty-three years old since I never travelled. One day the Lord spoke to me and told me to go to California. After getting confirmation from the Lord I told my wife and she said that I had to go if God had told me to. So I went. When I arrived back I did not expect the Lord to speak to me again about going overseas, but He kept sending me to different places. Go to Chicago. Go to Paris. Go to Geneva. I thought that it would be a short season, but it has turned out to be an ongoing season. I have been to sixty countries for the Lord and continue to travel after thirteen years in this season. I don't know if it will end. I just keep obeying Him.

In my travels I have seen so many wonderful things happen. Thousands of people have come to know Jesus Christ. Thousands have been healed and delivered of demons. Many marriages have been saved. Scores of people have been called into full-time ministry as a result. Many churches have been started. All because I obeyed the Lord.

When I first started to go, Ruth and I would make huge sacrifices financially and use all our month's salary to pay for a flight, then trust God for our daily food. We went through a season of this for about five years. Many of my trips have been to third world countries where they do not give you any offerings.

Also, when I started to travel, I would fly in economy class (coach class in the USA). I did that for seven years and over one hundred trips often involving up to twenty flights at a time. My back started to give me some trouble at the base of the spine and so I rebuked the pain, but it got worse. I was in pain for about six months. I asked God what was going on and He said this to me: "There are bigger seats on those planes you know!" I replied and said,

"Yes and do you know how much they cost!" The Lord spoke to my heart and said that if I would take the step of faith to fly business class then He would pay for it. It took a huge step of faith to do it, but I made a vow to God that I would never fly again in economy. I called my travel agent and told her to book my next trips all in business class. She said to me that I would have to pay about four times as much and I agreed. I only had about £50 when I booked that first business class fare and did not know where the money would come from.

In the next ten days over £4,000 came in from unexpected sources to pay for the flights which cost that much. That was four years ago and the money for my flights has come in more easily for business class than it ever did for economy class! Then last year God spoke to me again and said to start flying first class. My last four trips have all been in first class.

Let me explain something here. When you fly in economy class the effect on your body is quite considerable, particularly on long haul flights. In business class the effect on your body is reduced by 70%. I was much fresher to preach after travelling in business class on a long flight. It used to take me three days to recover from a long haul economy trip with the buzzing in my ears. In first class the effect is reduced by 90%. It is quite amazing. I can testify that the Lord has provided for all of this and continues to do so. Hallelujah! After all, we are kings and priests unto God and not paupers! Some of you simply need to take a step of faith. Thus I had a season of seven years in economy class, three years in business class and now my next season is in first class.

These two seasons of my life have turned out to be most influential for the kingdom and came totally out of the blue. You never know how the Lord will surprise you as you keep your heart with Him and seek His face.

CHAPTER 14

THE SEASONS
OF A
CHRISTIAN

We are all given grace to go through different seasons. God is with us whatever season we find ourselves in.

I have had many people tell me that I am wrong to travel so much and be away from my wife. What they are really saying is that they could not do it and would never have the faith for it. God always gives the grace to fulfil a particular calling. Such it is with us. Ruth and I are closer to each other today for having been through our tailor-made seasons. I grow more in love with Ruth each day and I think that being away from her from time to time has helped to draw us even closer.

Look at what the Word of God says:

> *"There hath no temptation taken you but such as is common to man: but God is faithful, who will not suffer you to be tempted above that ye are able; but will with the temptation also make a way to escape, that ye may be able to bear it."*
>
> (1 CORINTHIANS 10:13)

The word temptation here can also be translated as "trial" or "test" which gives a different slant to this verse.

Thus we can go through any season that comes our way with whatever trial or test it may bring, as God would not put us through something that was unbearable.

I know some people who have had to go through so many trials, I don't think that I could have endured them as well as they have. They have been given grace for their season.

This is where we also need to be careful not to judge each other, which can be a temptation for some.

> *"Judge not, that ye be not judged."*
>
> (MATTHEW 7:1)

> *"Judge not, and ye shall not be judged: condemn not, and ye shall not be condemned: forgive, and ye shall be forgiven."*
>
> (LUKE 6:37)

> *"Judge not according to the appearance, but judge righteous judgment."*
>
> (JOHN 7:24)

Also, we are each given differing faith levels to go with our particular calling, which can help to understand the varying seasons that we are called to.

> *"For I say, through the grace given unto me, to every man that is among you, not to think of himself more highly than he ought to think; but to think soberly, according as God hath dealt to every man the measure of faith."*
>
> (ROMANS 12:3)

This is a key scripture since we are given different tasks to perform in the kingdom which will require a different set of individual seasons of preparation to complete those tasks. We need to widen our understanding here and not be too narrow and thus condemning of others who do certain things in the kingdom.

We need to respect one another and pray for each other and thank God that we are not called to do something that we are not able to do!

> *"To speak evil of no man, to be no brawlers, but gentle, shewing all meekness unto all men."*
>
> (TITUS 3:2)

God calls many people to do some extraordinary things for Him and we should help such people in any way we can, even if we don't understand.

Just as in the armed forces, soldiers have to go through a season of training before they can engage in real combat, so it is with the Christian life. There are many seasons that we all have to go through to prepare us for some major battles.

I know that I could not be doing what I am doing today around the world without having gone through so many seasons.

On the last three international trips that I have been on I have been confronted by very strong demonic opposition and have had to deal with it. Territorial spirits have literally come to fight against me and tried to put fear on me. In each case I have overcome them by knowing what to do.

I was recently in Venezuela for the first time and was ministering in three different cities starting in the capital Caracas. There was much freedom to minister and signs and wonders broke out easily. Then I went to another city where again there was freedom. I then went to a third city where it was like walking through treacle in the heavenlies.

I got into the pulpit to preach, but it was very hard. All of a sudden I saw a prince of darkness come to attack me in the pulpit. I have never had it so vividly anywhere in the world. I was thrown into confusion for a moment. I decided to rebuke the spirit publicly and as I took authority over it many people got up and went out to the toilets and vomited!

I was due to speak at a national pastors and leaders' conference the next day, but when I arrived at the church I was called into the apostle's office. I was interrogated for over an hour about what I had done the night before. The guy asked me to apologise in front of his church for what I had done. I was very humble and submitted to his authority of course. I promised that I would apologise in front of his church on the Sunday morning as I was due to preach again.

It was like treading on egg shells for the next two days as I spoke to the pastors and prophets etc.

However, during those two days the people who had vomited into the toilets came up to the apostle one by one and told him that they had been healed of all sorts of long-term illnesses!

By the Sunday morning he did not want me to apologise but said that I could preach on anything that I wanted to, and do whatever God called me to do! Also, he asked, when was I coming back?! Hallelujah.

I could not have dealt with this sort of thing without going through many seasons of preparation. You never know what you are going to have to deal with next in my job.

I once was staying in a pastor's home in Florida where I was preaching for the whole weekend. It was a great church with about 700 people. I preached on the Saturday and then at the Sunday morning service and only had one meeting left before flying home to the UK. All that afternoon the Lord was speaking to me about the pastor's wife. God told me that I had to pray for her before leaving. I went up to her and asked if I could pray for her. She said "No!" I was younger than she was and I could sense her reticence at me even offering. God told me to ask her again. She said "No!" again. I asked her about five times if I could pray for her. God told me that it was vital that I ministered to her and so I eventually said in a loud voice, "Let me pray for you lady!" At that she said yes, but only after the service back at the home. It turned out that she was about the give up the ministry altogether as she had been hurt by so many people in the church.

As I prayed for her with her husband I could feel the power of God being poured into her and I rebuked all of the hurt. I kept my hands on her head for about one hour as God was doing so much in her. Afterwards she was delivered and threw her arms around her husband. I am so glad that I obeyed.

However, I could not have done that a few years ago. I have had to go through all kinds of seasons to get me to the place where I will do those kinds of things.

If you do not understand why you are going through a particular season then just keep trusting God. It will become evident one way or another, sooner or later. We have to learn to rejoice in whatever season we are in since it is simply preparation for the next season! That is for sure.

CHAPTER 15

UNNECESSARY SEASONS

It is true that we can learn things in any season about God or ourselves and even about life itself. However, it has to be said that some of us go through seasons that God never intended for us. The reasons for this kind of season could be many things. Here are a few to consider.

1. Rebellion
2. Plain old disobedience
3. Sin
4. Laziness

5. A wrong decision
6. Being wrongly influenced by others
7. Making choices under pressure
8. Fear

Adam was very content in the garden of Eden until one day Eve came along and offered him forbidden fruit. He was put under pressure by his wife who had been tempted by Satan and it led to his downfall. He was plunged into a season from which he could never recover or change. Not only did his rebellion put Adam and Eve into a dark season, but the whole human race! It is so amazing that one man can affect so many!

Praise God that Jesus came to bring us back again into fellowship with Him.

> *"For if by one man's offence death reigned by one; much more they which receive abundance of grace and of the gift of righteousness shall reign in life by one, Jesus Christ. Therefore as by the offence of one judgment came upon all men to condemnation; even so by the righteousness of one the free gift came upon all men unto justification of life. For as by one man's disobedience many were made sinners, so by the obedience of one shall many be made righteous."*
>
> (ROMANS 5:17–19)

Our job as Christians is to stay close to the Lord and to constantly seek His face so as not to go through a wrong season.

Never make any decision in your life when you are under pressure, or when you are tired or not totally sure that it is the will of God – particularly when it comes to choosing the person that you marry. You must be absolutely certain that he or she is the right person for you. If you have any doubts at all then do not marry! Wait until all of your doubts have been ironed out and if you are not sure, then you must not do it. You may find yourself in a season that prevents you from fulfilling the plan and purpose of God for your life. Maybe God wants you to be single to do His work? Perhaps He has somebody else lined up for you that you have not even met yet. I believe that many have entered into marriage far too quickly and if only they had waited a bit longer to make sure it would have saved them from a bad season.

Having said this, if you have already made that decision to marry then your job is to make the very best of what you have and trust God to make it better.

Job went into a season of his life that was not the perfect will of God for him at all. He was a godly man who was right with God, but he was in fear for his children and kept making the same sacrifices for them.

"And it was so, when the days of their feasting were gone about, that Job sent and sanctified them, and rose up early in the morning, and offered burnt offerings according to the number of them all: **for Job said, It may be that my sons have sinned, and cursed God in their hearts. Thus did Job continually.**"

(JOB 1:5)

"It may be" means that Job was guessing and it was based on fear and worry.

Look at what Job admits later on:

"For the thing which I greatly feared is come upon me, and that which I was afraid of is come unto me."

(JOB 3:25)

Job then had dozens of chapters recording a season that need not have taken place!

I wonder how many seasons we go through that we should never have gone through? Just think about your own life.

Having said that, God is bigger than our mistakes and shortcomings and can use even our mistakes to bring us on in Him. He can use any situation that we find ourselves in to refine us and shape us.

But I would rather find the perfect will of God for my life, not have to go through any more unnecessary seasons, and just fulfil His will each day.

What about you?

This prompts the obvious question: suppose we realise that we are currently in such a season. How do we get out of it?

The sooner we learn to rejoice in our present season the sooner we will come out of it! If you have sinned then you need to repent. Some sins carry a season of the indignation of the Lord. But God can and will get you out in His time.

"Rejoice not against me, O mine enemy: when I fall, I shall arise; when I sit in darkness, the LORD shall be a light unto me. I will bear the indignation of the LORD, because I have sinned

against him, until he plead my cause, and execute judgment for me: he will bring me forth to the light, and I shall behold his righteousness."

(MICAH 7:8–9)

CHAPTER 16

DWELLING ON PAST SEASONS

It is interesting in the Christian life that we often learn more through a tough season than through an easy one. We have to use our faith more and depend more on the Lord. It is usually harder to stay close to the Lord in a fruitful season without any opposition.

I can look back at my Christian life, at the many seasons that the Lord has brought me through. Some were really difficult and others were full of blessing. However, they have all ceased and many new seasons have taken their place.

I have met some lovely Christians who dwell on a past season as if it were yesterday, just because it was so good. They don't talk about the present at all, but are locked in the past in "the good old days". This is a very dangerous place to be, because what they are actually saying is that God is not doing anything today! That is very wrong and if you have been caught up in dwelling on past blessings then repent and move on. God has even better days ahead for you if you will believe Him.

Also, some dwell on a really difficult season in their life when they had a tough time and they keep going back to that season. They have not moved on. We need to learn from the past but keeping moving forward!

*"Brethren, I count not myself to have apprehended: but this one thing I do, **forgetting those things which are behind, and reaching forth unto those things which are before.***"

(PHILIPPIANS 3:13)

"Then shall we know, if we follow on to know the LORD: his going forth is prepared as the morning; and he shall come unto us as the rain, as the latter and former rain unto the earth."

(HOSEA 6:3)

We need to look ahead with eager anticipation for what the Lord is going to bring in the next season of life. Yes, we can learn from past blessings and failures but we must not be restricted or intimidated by the past.

"Now unto him that is able to do exceeding abundantly above all that we ask or think, according to the power that worketh in us."

(EPHESIANS 3:20)

We need to clear our hearts of the past and set our goal on the future where God can do even more for us than He has ever done before. We are hopefully wiser than we were before and so the Lord can entrust us with a fruitful season.

Don't dwell on the past at all. Run the race that is set before you.

"Wherefore seeing we also are compassed about with so great a cloud of witnesses, **let us lay aside every weight, and the sin which doth so easily beset us, and let us run with patience the race that is set before us, looking unto Jesus the author and finisher of our faith; who for the joy that was set before him endured the cross, despising the shame, and is set down at the right hand of the throne of God."**

(HEBREWS 12:1–2)

This passage helps us to put our lives into perspective by catching a glimpse of eternity. We are being made ready for the best season ever – with Jesus in heaven! If all we ever focus on is down here on Earth then we will be very limited indeed. We shall all be in heaven shortly and then all of the seasons, the good, bad and indifferent, will be forgotten and we shall be able to worship the Lamb upon the throne with thousands of millions of others from all over the world together in harmony. What a season that will be!

Some think that heaven is going to be boring with nothing to do. Are you one of them? I don't think so somehow. I once heard a sermon about heaven that blessed me so much. The preacher shared that in heaven there will be an ever-revealing series of new seasons to enjoy. Each age bringing a new season of joy to us. It is not going to be flat, level and boring at all! It will be amazing since God is the author of it. Just look at how varied your seasons have been on this Earth! I am quite sure that heaven will be awesome in wonder, splendour, joy, freedom, creative expression etc. It will be many times more wonderful than this world that is for sure.

This should be motivating to you to live this life in victory and to overcome all that the devil throws at you.

Also, remember that in the Christian life it is not how you start that matters, but HOW YOU FINISH! It is a long race with many twists and turns producing many challenges to us. Then, when you think that you have seen it all, you enter a new season which stretches your faith beyond anything you have ever seen before! What a mighty God we serve.

CHAPTER 17

THE SEASONS OF THE CHURCH

"And I say also unto thee, That thou art Peter, and upon this rock I will build my church; and the gates of hell shall not prevail against it."

(MATTHEW 16:18)

The church of Jesus Christ is bigger and stronger today than it has ever been and yet it has been through so many different seasons! Ruth and I were on holiday in Turkey last year and we were able to visit Ephesus. It was amazing!

In fact all seven of the churches of Asia are situated in modern-day Turkey. Paul worked so hard to build these churches up and yet there is nothing left today! They had their season. Now the church is growing in some countries of the world so fast that it would dwarf the early Church. In Mozambique for instance there are tens of thousands of churches all over the place. In Nigeria the Christians are running the Muslims out of the country there are so many of them. In fact the largest church in the world is in Nigeria with over one million members!

I have recently been out to preach in South Korea where they have had a revival for the past thirty-five years which has now stopped. It was a season of growth in the Church that has been spoken about the world over, but they are now looking for the next season. I will be out there soon to speak at two conferences on apostolic ministry and there is such a hunger for a new wave of the anointing of God's Spirit.

Over the last thirty years there have been different seasons that have moved upon the Church worldwide for those that would embrace them. In the 1970s there was the season of charismatic renewal that impacted many denominational churches. During the 1980s we saw a season of "Word of Faith" teaching which brought a strong emphasis on atonement healing, victorious living and prosperity. Then in the 1990s there was another season with an emphasis upon prophetic ministry and the restoration of the office of the prophet back to the church. There was also a refreshing wave which some called the "Toronto Blessing" where holy laughter spread across the global Church.

At the turn of the millennium there was another season released upon the Church which is the restoration of the apostle. Everywhere I go these days people are asking about the ministry of the apostle. Countless books are being written all across the globe as God has brought a new season upon His Church. I personally believe that we should embrace all that God does in and through His Body. We need prophets, we need victory, we need holiness, we need holy laughter, we need prosperity and we need apostles! Many have resisted some or all of these revelations that the Holy Spirit has brought in these last days, but I strongly believe that we need everything that the Holy Spirit wants to do, both to prepare for an outpouring of the Spirit upon the Earth, as well as to mature us for our eternal future.

There are also seasons that an individual church goes through. It was nearly fifteen years ago that Ruth and I started Life Changing Ministries from nothing as a pioneer work. The first four years were so difficult. People coming and going, letting us down etc. It did not look like a church at all. They were mostly broken and hurting people with lots of baggage from the past. Many had been married several times, some had been in and out of mental hospitals and one was still a Satanist! Almost all of them were broke including us! What a formula for starting anything! All I had was a word from God!

I was reading about Solomon one day and a verse just leapt out at me:

*"In the **fourth year was the foundation of the house of the** Lord **laid**, in the month Zif: and **in the eleventh***

*year, in the month Bul, which is the eighth month, **was the house finished throughout all the parts thereof,** and according to all the fashion of it. So was he seven years in building it."*

(1 KINGS 6:37–38)

The Lord spoke to my heart from these scriptures and said that it takes four years to build the foundation and another seven years to build up the walls – eleven years in total until the house will be finished. A four-year season, then a seven-year season makes eleven years. What a long time to get anything established.

However, I can now testify that it did take four years to get the foundation in place and then another seven-year season before the house was built, so to speak. In the twelfth year of Life Changing Ministries we began to see some real breakthroughs and in the last two years it has increased more and more.

Our whole ministry has entered a new season of real blessing that is beyond our expectations!

We had to go through so much to come into our present season of harvest and blessing and God is continuing to bless us now. The mother church keeps getting stronger and more churches are joining us all the time. Our churches in other countries keep reporting breakthroughs with other new churches springing up. Hallelujah! I like this season! Long may it continue.

Another season that we went through in our mother church that nearly destroyed LCM altogether was the season of Jezebel. I have to mention this since I hear about this menace regularly.

I confess that I had never encountered the Jezebel spirit before in all three churches that I had led. Or should I say that I had not recognised it before. But we had a wave of ladies that turned out to be Jezebel's. There were five in all; one after the other and all totally different in personality. They were not all obvious, but they all sought to control me in some way. We tried in vain to cast out the spirit of Jezebel from some of them. Sadly, I have to report that none of the five came through. They all ended up leaving our ministry. Let me explain something here. A woman can have a controlling tendency and repent. What I am talking about is a full manifestation of Jezebel that has no intention of changing.

I remember one Sunday morning after the service had ended that the first Jezebel we had went up to Ruth and told her that I was not called to lead the church at all, but I was trying to build my own kingdom. She was trying to divide me and Ruth. I sent her a letter and told her that we were prepared to minister deliverance to her and we never saw her again! Then she turned up in one of our other churches in a different town and she spoke to the leaders, attacking me. I had already warned them about her and they threw her out. That was about twelve years ago. I have just heard that this same woman has just destroyed a church in our city and tried to discredit a godly man.

During this season of dealing with Jezebel the Lord spoke to me and told me that it is not a spirit of Jezebel, but a woman Jezebel! Look at the Scriptures:

*"**Notwithstanding I have a few things against thee, because thou sufferest that woman Jezebel, which calleth herself a prophetess, to teach and to seduce my***

servants to commit fornication, *and to eat things sacrificed unto idols."*

(REVELATION 2:20)

God said to me that I should have zero tolerance from now on regarding this kind of woman. We are not to tolerate Jezebel but expose her and confront her and if she does not repent then we need to get rid of her and warn others also.

We speak about it from the front and warn all of our ladies to be on their guard in their own life and also in others. It can destroy much good and as leaders, we are responsible.

This verse also says that she calls herself a prophetess. That is one of the obvious signs of Jezebel, when someone claims to be a prophetess. If you are called as a prophetess then you need to wait for others to confirm it rather than parade it to everyone!

This verse also tells us about the sexual side of Jezebel that we all need to watch out for.

As I have travelled around and talked to different leaders about this subject it seems that Jezebel usually attacks apostles more than anyone. Probably because it is the hardest thing to deal with.

If you have not had to deal with this horrible situation as yet then you may have to before long.

Some have asked me if I think that Jezebel is just in women. My answer is yes. It is a different spirit in men. I believe that it is the Absalom spirit which works through men to seek to control and try to take over. We have had both in our ministry, but it has been Jezebel that has been by far the worst.

"And there came a messenger to David, saying, The hearts of the men of Israel are after Absalom. And David said unto all his servants that were with him at Jerusalem, Arise, and let us flee; for we shall not else escape from Absalom: make speed to depart, lest he overtake us suddenly, and bring evil upon us, and smite the city with the edge of the sword."

(2 SAMUEL 15:13–14)

As leaders we have to watch out for those who would try to take over from us and destroy the work of God.

I learnt so much from that season of Jezebel in our church and I have been able to warn so many. I have also seen it so many times even in big churches where the senior pastor is being controlled by his wife!

You have been warned!

CHAPTER 18

FINANCIAL SEASONS

We all have to deal with money every day of our lives. It is an interesting subject to talk about since it can change so quickly! Many people go through a season where they don't have much at all and have to trust daily for their basic needs. I have been there for many years in the past where we had to trust God for our daily food. We were happy and rejoicing knowing that we were doing the will of God. I would rather have nothing and be doing God's will than have millions in the bank and be out of Father's will! However, there is another step in that equation and that is to have plenty of money *and* stay in the will of God. As one preacher once said, "It does not matter how much money you have in ministry you can always use more!" That is true. There is always something that needs to be replaced, more air time on TV, more flights to pay for, more books to publish etc.

Do not think that having lots of money can make you happy either. If you do have lots of it you will know what I mean. It brings more responsibility to use it wisely. It can happen to you just like that. In a short time you could be left hundreds of thousands of pounds in a will for instance. It has been known to ruin some people who have not been used to having money before. It takes a great amount of wisdom to handle money properly. Some people become guilty of spending any money on themselves which is wrong. Provided that you have tithed correctly and given when God told you to give, then enjoy some of it yourself. You don't have to give it all away!

One day Joseph was given a revelation from God about one of Pharaoh's dreams.

"And Joseph said unto Pharaoh, The dream of Pharaoh is one: God hath shewed Pharaoh what he is about to do. The seven good kine are seven years; and the seven good ears are seven years: the dream is one. And the seven thin and ill favoured kine that came up after them are seven years; and the seven empty ears blasted with the east wind shall be seven years of famine. This is the thing which I have spoken unto Pharaoh: What God is about to do he sheweth unto Pharaoh. Behold, there come seven years of great plenty throughout all the land of Egypt: And there shall arise after them seven years of famine; and all the plenty

shall be forgotten in the land of Egypt; and the famine shall consume the land."

(GENESIS 41:25–30)

Those of you who know your Bible will remember the story. Maybe you want to refresh your memory by reading it again. Joseph interpreted Pharaoh's dream and told him that they were going to have seven years of abundant harvest followed by seven years of famine. What a revelation! It helped them to know how to plan for it and to save some resources for the coming famine. If we would only listen to the Lord He can tell us similar things today in the financial realm as well as every other area. God is interested in every part of life and can guide us and warn us by speaking through prophets. The Lord talks to me regularly about finances since I have to believe Him for so much these days.

I believe that if we are doing the will of God, obeying Him at all times, tithing and sowing seeds into good ground and submitting to those in authority over us then we will have an ever increasing harvest, so that we can fulfil our destiny and purpose on the Earth.

However, the Scriptures warn us that when wealth does come our way we must keep seeking God's face and going on with Him. We must never trust in money since it can easily go away again!

"Charge them that are rich in this world, that they be not highminded, nor trust in uncertain riches, but in the living God, who giveth us richly all things to enjoy; that they do good, that they be rich in good works, ready to distribute, willing to communicate;

laying up in store for themselves a good foundation against the time to come, that they may lay hold on eternal life."

(1 TIMOTHY 6:17–19)

"And it shall be, when the LORD thy God shall have brought thee into the land which he sware unto thy fathers, to Abraham, to Isaac, and to Jacob, to give thee great and goodly cities, which thou buildedst not, and houses full of all good things, which thou filledst not, and wells digged, which thou diggedst not, vineyards and olive trees, which thou plantedst not; when thou shalt have eaten and be full; then beware lest thou forget the LORD, which brought thee forth out of the land of Egypt, from the house of bondage. Thou shalt fear the LORD thy God, and serve him, and shalt swear by his name."

(DEUTERONOMY 6:10–13)

"When thou hast eaten and art full, then thou shalt bless the LORD thy God for the good land which he hath given thee.

Beware that thou forget not the LORD thy God, in not keeping his commandments, and his judgments, and his statutes, which I command thee this day: **Lest when thou hast eaten and art full, and hast built goodly houses, and dwelt therein; And when thy herds and thy flocks multiply, and thy silver and thy gold is multiplied, and all that thou hast is multiplied; Then thine heart be lifted up, and thou forget the LORD thy God, which brought thee forth out of the land of Egypt, from the house of bondage;** *Who led thee through that great and terrible wilderness, wherein were fiery serpents, and scorpions, and drought, where there was no water; who brought thee forth water out of the rock of flint; Who fed thee in the wilderness with* *manna, which thy fathers knew not, that he might humble thee, and that he might prove thee, to do thee good at thy latter end; And thou say in thine heart, My power and the might of mine hand hath gotten me this wealth.*

But thou shalt remember the LORD thy God: for it is he that giveth thee power to get wealth, that he may establish his covenant which he sware unto thy fathers, as it is this day.

And it shall be, if thou do at all forget the LORD thy God, and walk after other gods, and serve them, and worship them, I testify against you this day that ye shall surely perish."

(DEUTERONOMY 8:10–19)

"Trust not in oppression, and become not vain in robbery: **if riches increase, set not your heart upon them.***"*

(PSALM 62:10)

Our heart must ever be towards the Lord even if you become a millionaire. We need people with vast amounts of money to fund the gospel in the last days. Pray for God to raise up such people who will continue to lead godly lives and you might become one of them!

Also, if you have a season of lack in this area then you are more likely to appreciate it than someone who has always had plenty. I pray that you have a seasonal change financially for the sake of the kingdom of God.

"Thou hast caused men to ride over our heads; we went through fire and through water: but thou broughtest us out into a wealthy place."

(PSALM 66:12)

A good season often follows a hard season! I trust that this brings you hope.

Remember that all seasons come to an end. Whatever they may be. So always be on your guard and don't become complacent in your relationship with God. Spend time with Him and continue to grow in His goodness.

CHAPTER 19

A REASON
FOR THE
SEASON!

We do not always understand why we find ourselves in a particular season until after it is long finished.

Joseph went through a very interesting season that we can all learn from. I am sure that while he was going through it he questioned why it was all happening. His own brothers sold him as a slave after almost killing him! All because of jealousy brought on by his father. We should all love our children equally and not spoil one above another.

Joseph eventually finds himself in Egypt bought by Potiphar.

"And the LORD was with Joseph, and he was a prosperous man; and he was in the house of his master the Egyptian. And his master saw that the LORD was with him, and that the LORD made all that he did to prosper in his hand. And Joseph found grace in his sight, and he served him: and he made him overseer over his house, and all that he had he put into his hand.

And it came to pass from the time that he had made him overseer in his house, and over all that he had, that the LORD blessed the Egyptian's house for Joseph's sake; and the blessing of the LORD was upon all that he had in the house, and in the field. And he left all that he had in Joseph's hand; and he knew not ought he had, save the bread which he did eat. And Joseph was a goodly person, and well favoured.

And it came to pass after these things, that his master's wife cast her eyes upon Joseph; and she said, Lie with me. But he refused, and said unto his master's wife, Behold, my master wotteth not what is with me in the house, and he hath committed all that he hath to my hand."

(GENESIS 39:2–8)

You can read the rest of the story for yourself. Joseph gets falsely accused of raping his master's wife and is thrown into prison. He kept prospering because he was innocent and right with God. He even prospered in the prison!

"And Joseph's master took him, and put him into the prison, a place where the king's prisoners were bound: and he was there in the prison. But the LORD was with Joseph, and shewed him

mercy, and gave him favour in the sight of the keeper of the prison. And the keeper of the prison committed to Joseph's hand all the prisoners that were in the prison; and whatsoever they did there, he was the doer of it. The keeper of the prison looked not to any thing that was under his hand; because the LORD was with him, and that which he did, the LORD made it to prosper."

(GENESIS 39:20–23)

God was preparing his man for something very special although Joseph was oblivious to it at this time. He needed some rough edges smoothed off him in order to fulfil the purpose of God. God knows what it takes to refine us ready for our eventual destiny. Joseph could never have imagined the significance of his life at this point.

He still needed two more years after the butler and baker situation until his heart was ready for the next season.

Let us look at Joseph's promotion from the Word of God:

"And Pharaoh said unto his servants, Can we find such a one as this is, a man in whom the Spirit of God is?

And Pharaoh said unto Joseph, Forasmuch as God hath shewed thee all this, there is none so discreet and wise as thou art: Thou shalt be over my house, and according unto thy word shall all my people be ruled: only in the throne will I be greater than thou.

And Pharaoh said unto Joseph, See, I have set thee over all the land of Egypt.

And Pharaoh took off his ring from his hand, and put it upon Joseph's hand, and arrayed him in vestures of fine linen, and put a gold chain about his neck; And he made him to ride

in the second chariot which he had; and they cried before him,
Bow the knee: and he made him ruler over all the land of
Egypt."

(GENESIS 41:38–43)

Joseph was given the second chariot in Egypt! He became
the saviour of so many. He entered a season that most
people could not even have imagined. He also realised that
God was in it otherwise he could have taken vengeance on
his brothers who tried to kill him. He was not bitter since he
recognised that God had raised him up for "such a time as
this"!

"And his brethren also went and fell down before his face; and
they said, Behold, we be thy servants. And Joseph said unto
them, Fear not: for am I in the place of God? **But as for you,**
ye thought evil against me; but God meant it unto
good, to bring to pass, as it is this day, to save much
people alive."

(GENESIS 50:18–20)

This story is so powerful and so encouraging, particularly
when we are going through a hard season. I have held onto
this story of Joseph many times in my life believing that my
life might mean something one day.

Seasons:
1. Every season is a chance for us to grow.
2. God is in charge of our seasons and we need to trust
   Him.
3. Every season is temporary and subject to change.

4. We need to rejoice in every season and overcome it.
5. We need a new release of faith for each season.
6. Your present season is a preparation for the next one.
7. God is with you in every season.
8. The best season is yet to be!
9. The Lord can surprise you with a new season at any time.
10. Our eternal season in heaven is not too far away.

Hallelujah!

CHAPTER 20

WHEN A SEASON CHANGES

I know what it is like to be right in the middle of a fruitful season where your faith is being stretched and you don't have time for anything else. You are not even thinking about the next season at all, but simply getting on with it.

I can remember years ago that the Lord gave me a mandate to go to every major capital city of the world and engage in spiritual warfare. This word was given to me on the TGV train from Paris to Geneva. I can remember it as if it was yesterday, it was so clear. Over the next eight years the Lord took me all over the world praying in high places in cities such as New York, Moscow, Paris, Kingston, Cairo, Jerusalem, London, Prague, Bratislava, Bermuda, Los Angeles, Bogota, Buenos Aires, Seoul, Tokyo, Colombo, Kathmandu, Istanbul, Vienna, Berlin, Stockholm, Oslo, Chicago, Madrid, Reykjavik, Singapore, Bangkok, Sydney and Johannesburg.

One day as I was engaging in spiritual warfare in Seoul, Korea something lifted off me while in a bus. It was the burden that I had been carrying for spiritual warfare for eight years. It just lifted off me and I knew that I had fulfilled that part of my life. Many of those countries that I prayed in over those years have since invited me back to preach there. Hallelujah.

It always feels strange when a season lifts off you. I always feel like I am in shallow water which is not where I like to be at all. I like to get my "faith teeth" into something and take on a new challenge. I suppose that is why I am an apostle. Some people can't stand new challenges by nature of their calling, but I love it. Blazing a new trail is right up my street.

Another thing that often happens to me before a new season starts is that I become pregnant with something. This happened at the start of this year (2005). I could feel myself getting into shallow water and wanting a new challenge. I then sensed that I was feeling pregnant in my spirit with something new, but did not know what it was. So I went away to pray about it and I think that the Lord has shown me the next step in a particular part of my life that I cannot divulge as yet.

It is as if I am about to give birth to something that is inside of me into the spirit realm. I hope you can understand that as I am doing my very best to explain it!

Now, what do we do when we know that a season is changing but we are not sure what it is yet? It is a good question and I have a very simple answer. You must do nothing at all! You have to wait until God has clearly shown you what the next step is or else you will make a mess of it.

This is where patience is needed. You need to pray and seek the Lord for guidance and He will show you. Never act out of desperation, but out of direction. God will show you in time. Things have a habit of coming into focus with the passage of time. Seasons will come and seasons will go and it is often a challenge to our faith in a season change to simply stand still and see what God does.

Also, some seasons take much longer than we expect when they begin. I have been surprised at how long I have been in a season of change before the next season emerges. It usually takes a step of faith on my part when I am nearing the end of such a time and so I spend much time listening to the Holy Spirit and staying close to what He says to me. We are only responsible for the next step! That is so comforting. Don't try to work it all out in your mind or else you will get brain cramps!

OTHER BOOKS BY TREVOR NEWPORT

What the Bible Says About YOUR Provision and Prosperity
Did You Go OR Were You Sent? (An autobiography)
King Jesus is Coming Soon!
Angels, Demons and Spiritual Warfare
The Ministry of Jesus Christ
Divine Appointments
The Two U's: Unbelief and Unforgiveness
Secrets of Success
From Victory to Victory
Pitfalls in Ministry
How to Pray in the Spirit
The Anointing: the Vital Ingredient
A Practical Guide to Fasting

Prophets, Prophesying and Personal Prophecy
Absolute Faith
As Jesus Is, So Are We in This World
Sharpening Iron: Developing Godly Relationships
Healing, Health and Wholeness
Present Day Miracles
Signs, Wonders and Miracles

FURTHER
INFORMATION

If you would like to contact Trevor Newport for any aspect
of ministry then please write to:

Life Changing Ministries Headquarters
Bemersley House
Gitana Street
Hanley, Stoke on Trent
Staffordshire
ST1 1DY
United Kingdom

We hope you enjoyed reading this New Wine book.
For details of other New Wine books
and a range of 2,000 titles from other
Spirit-filled publishers visit our website:
www.newwineministries.co.uk